Lucy Maud Montgomery

With thanks and admiration to "kindred spirit" Donna Jane Campbell for all she does to promote the love of Maud's work. — E.M.

For Leanne — J.M.

The publisher and author wish to express their gratitude and appreciation to Dr. Elizabeth Epperly for her review of the book. While every effort has been made to ensure accuracy, any errors are the responsibility of the author and publisher.

L.M. Montgomery is a trademark of Heirs of L.M. Montgomery Inc.

Anne of Green Gables and other indicia of "Anne" are trademarks and Canadian official marks of the Anne of Green Gables Licensing Authority Inc.

® Kids Can Read is a registered trademark of Kids Can Press Ltd.

Kids Can Press acknowledges the financial support of the Government of Ontario, through the Ontario Media Development Corporation's Ontario Book Initiative; the Ontario Arts Council; the Canada Council for the Arts; and the Government of Canada, through the BPIDP, for our publishing activity.

Published in Canada by	Published in the U.S. by
Kids Can Press Ltd.	Kids Can Press Ltd.
29 Birch Avenue	2250 Military Road
Toronto, ON M4V 1E2	Tonawanda, NY 14150

www.kidscanpress.com

Edited by David MacDonald
Designed by Marie Bartholomew
Printed and bound in Singapore
Educational consultant: Maureen Skinner Weiner, United Synagogue Day School, Willowdale, Ontario.

The hardcover edition of this book is smyth sewn casebound.
The paperback edition of this book is limp sewn with a drawn-on cover.

CM 08 0 9 8 7 6 5 4 3 2 1
CM PA 08 0 9 8 7 6 5 4 3 2 1

Library and Archives Canada Cataloguing in Publication
MacLeod, Elizabeth 3/08

    Lucy Maud Montgomery / written by Elizabeth MacLeod ; illustrated by John Mantha.

(Kids Can read)
ISBN 978-1-55453-055-7 (bound)   ISBN 978-1-55453-056-4 (pbk.)

1. Montgomery, L. M. (Lucy Maud), 1874–1942—Juvenile literature.
2. Novelists, Canadian (English) —20th century—Biography—Juvenile literature. I. Mantha, John II. Title. III. Series: Kids Can read (Toronto, Ont.)

PS8526.O55Z793 2008   jC813'.52   C2007-902702-4

Kids Can Press is a **l⊙rUS**™ Entertainment company

Lucy Maud Montgomery

Written by Elizabeth MacLeod
Illustrated by John Mantha

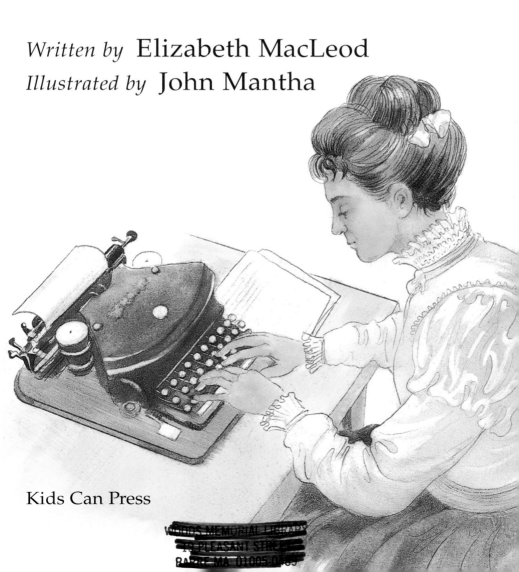

Kids Can Press

Have you ever dreamed of writing a book? Have you wondered what it would be like to be famous for the books you wrote?

When Lucy Maud Montgomery was a young girl, she dreamed of writing books. She grew up and wrote about a girl named Anne. Anne lived in a house that was called Green Gables.

The books about Anne of Green Gables made Lucy Maud Montgomery one of the most famous writers in the world.

Lucy Maud Montgomery was born on Prince Edward Island, Canada, in 1874. She hated the name Lucy, so she asked people to call her Maud.

Maud always made sure people spelled her name correctly—without an "e" at the end.

Before Maud was two years old, her mother died. Her father had to move far away to get a job.

Maud lived in Cavendish, Prince Edward Island, with her grandparents. They expected her to always be very good and quiet.

Maud was often sad and lonely. To make herself feel better, she wrote short stories and poems.

Maud made up stories about her dolls, her cats and her favorite places. She wrote about things that happened at school. Maud loved writing.

When Maud was almost 16, a newspaper printed one of her poems. She was so happy! After that, Maud began to write even more.

Soon Maud's short stories and poems were in many newspapers and magazines.

A few years later, Maud moved away to study to become a teacher. But she always made time for writing.

Even after Maud started teaching, she woke up early in the morning so she could write before school.

In the winter, Maud's bedroom was very cold. Sometimes snow would blow in through cracks around her window onto her pillow.

Maud had to wear her heavy winter coat to stay warm while she was writing.

Maud's grandfather died in 1898. Her grandmother was too old to live alone. Maud gave up teaching. She moved back to Cavendish to stay with her grandmother.

Maud cooked and cleaned and looked after her grandmother. She helped her grandmother run the town's post office. It was in her grandmother's kitchen. Maud sold stamps for letters and packages.

Even though she was busy, Maud didn't stop writing. Now she was trying to get her poems and short stories in magazines that printed only the best writing.

Soon some of these magazines were printing Maud's poems and stories.

For a long time, Maud had wanted to write a book. But she could never think of a story idea that seemed good enough for a whole book.

One day, Maud was looking through an old notebook. In it, she had saved her ideas for stories and poems.

One of Maud's story ideas was about an older couple looking for a boy to help with chores. Instead, the couple ends up with a girl.

Right away, Maud began to plan a story about these people.

Maud could see in her mind what the girl looked like. She had bright red hair.

Maud named the girl Anne. Like Maud, Anne would make sure people knew how to spell her name. Maud decided that Anne could tell people her name was "Anne-with-an-e."

Maud thought Anne and the older couple might live in a house like one that was near hers.

This house had a green gable. A gable is the triangle-shaped part of a wall that touches the roof. Maud decided that the house in her story would be called Green Gables.

Maud thought up lots of adventures that Anne and her friends could have.

Did Maud finally have an idea that was good enough for a whole book?

One spring evening in May 1905, Maud began Anne's story. She loved writing about this young girl.

Maud wrote in the kitchen. She sat on the table, close to the window. The setting sun lit the pages as she worked.

Every day while she washed the dishes, Maud planned what Anne would do. When Maud hung out laundry, she decided what Anne would say.

That saved time for Maud. When she sat down to write, she knew exactly what would happen next in Anne's story.

All summer long, Maud wrote about Anne. Maud did most of her writing in the evening, after all of her other work was done.

In October, Maud finally finished writing *Anne of Green Gables*.

Maud carefully typed out her story. She wrapped up the pages. Then she mailed them off to a company that printed and sold books.

Maud quickly heard back from the company. The people there did not want to print her book.

So Maud sent her book to another company. That company did not like the book.

Maud mailed her book to three more companies. They all said no.

   After she had cried a little, Maud put
her story in an old hat box. She hid the
box away in her cupboard.

   Maud tried to forget about the book.
Maybe poems and short stories were all
that she was good at writing.

A few months later, Maud was cleaning out her cupboard. She opened a box and there was her book.

Maud began to read it again. "Maybe I can turn parts of it into short stories," she thought.

As Maud kept reading, she became more and more excited. "This *is* a good book," she told herself. "I am going to send it off to one more company."

Would this company think Maud's book was good enough?

On April 15, 1907, Maud got a letter. It was from the company she had sent her book to. Maud quickly opened the letter.

The company liked her book!

Finally Maud's story about Anne of Green Gables would be sold in stores. Maud's dream had come true.

About a year later, a very special package arrived for Maud. Her hands shook as she undid the wrapping. At last, there was a printed copy of her book, *Anne of Green Gables*. Maud was thrilled.

Maud went on to write many more books, and hundreds of short stories and poems. Eight of her books are about Anne and her family.

Maud won many prizes for her writing.
She became famous all around the world.

Today, people still love Maud's books.
Most of all, they love the stories about a
red-haired girl named "Anne-with-an-e."

More facts about Maud

• Lucy Maud Montgomery was born on November 30, 1874. She died on April 24, 1942.

• Maud wrote a total of 24 books, and hundreds of short stories and poems.

• On Prince Edward Island, you can visit the house that gave Maud the idea for Green Gables.

• Maud loved cats. There are cats in many of her books and stories.